Stop Smoking

A Comprehensive Handbook On Effectively And
Sustainably Overcoming Chronic Smoking Addictions
And Habits In A Natural Manner, Permanently

*(Cease The Habit Of Smoking Permanently And The Most
Effortless Method To Ultimately Renounce Smoking)*

Larry Meyer

TABLE OF CONTENT

Conquering Temptations: Strategies And Approaches For Achieving Triumph 1

Smoking's Endgame 21

Obstacles Encountered During The Cessation Of Smoking 46

Strategies For Achieving Long-Term Smoking Cessation. 76

What Is The Financial Revenue Generated By The Tobacco Industry? 94

Beginning To Comprehend The Addictive Substance 120

Conquer Withdrawal Symptoms And Cravings 151

The Adverse Consequences Of Smoking And The Rationale For Smoking Cessation 161

Conquering Temptations: Strategies And Approaches For Achieving Triumph

Desires can present a significant hindrance when endeavoring to attain objectives related to one's health and overall well-being. The process of overcoming cravings can be arduous when attempting to achieve various objectives such as weight loss, smoking cessation, or reducing sugar consumption. Presented below are several guidelines and strategies to effectively manage and conquer cravings:

Gain Awareness of Your Triggers: Cravings frequently originate from specific triggers, such as stress, monotony, or particular environmental stimuli. Determine the stimuli that elicit a response and make an effort to mitigate or control their occurrence to the greatest extent feasible.

Maintain Consistent Eating Habits: Adhering to a schedule of regularly consuming meals and snacks throughout the day can effectively ward off hunger and stabilize blood sugar levels, thereby mitigating cravings.

Maintain Adequate Hydration: Occasionally, thirst may be misinterpreted as hunger or food cravings. It is important to ensure adequate hydration by consuming ample amounts of water throughout the day in order to maintain proper bodily functions and prevent superfluous cravings.

Ensure Adequate Rest: Insufficient sleep has the potential to disrupt hormonal balance and trigger an increase in appetite, thereby encouraging cravings. Strive to achieve a minimum of 7-8 hours of sleep on a nightly basis in order to effectively regulate hormones and diminish cravings.

Redirect Your Attention: When faced with a craving, endeavor to redirect your focus by participating in an alternative activity, such as taking a stroll, immersing yourself in a novel, or reaching out to a companion through a phone call.

Engage in Mindfulness: Adopting mindfulness practices, such as employing deep breathing exercises, engaging in meditation, or participating in yoga, can effectively diminish stress levels and enhance self-awareness. This, in turn, is conducive to minimizing cravings.

Maintain a Stock of Nutritious Snacks: By ensuring the presence of wholesome snacks, one can effectively stave off any inclination towards unhealthy cravings. Select snack options that possess substantial amounts of protein, fiber, and nourishing fats, such as nuts, seeds, fruits, and vegetables.

Appeal for Assistance: Acquiring assistance from acquaintances, relatives, or a support network can foster your determination and responsibility, while offering uplifting encouragement during moments of adversity.

Recognize and Substitute Detrimental Patterns: Longings can similarly arise from unfavorable routines, such as consuming unhealthy snacks while engaged in television viewing or engaging in smoking during work breaks. Identify these habits and substitute them with more wholesome alternatives, such as consuming fruit as a snack or engaging in a brief walk during your designated break time.

Incorporate Visualization Techniques: The integration of visualization techniques has proven to be effective in conquering cravings. Envision yourself attaining your objectives and contemplate the emotions that will arise once you have successfully conquered your desires. This can assist in maintaining your motivation and adherence to the designated path.

Exercise Self-Restraint: Fully abstaining from indulging in your cravings can potentially amplify their allure. Rather than entirely removing specific foods or activities, adopt a moderate approach and permit yourself occasional small indulgences.

Maintain an optimistic mindset: Engaging in positive thoughts can truly exert a profound influence on your capacity to surmount urges. Place emphasis on your accomplishments rather than your shortcomings, and consistently reinforce the strides you have taken towards achieving your objectives.

Reap the Fruits of Your Efforts: Commemorate your achievements by indulging in a well-deserved treat that coincides with your objectives. This can aid in the strengthening of positive conduct and sustain your motivation.

Avail oneself of professional assistance: In instances where one experiences challenges in conquering cravings or contends with addiction, it may be imperative to solicit professional intervention. A healthcare practitioner can furnish assistance, counsel, and provisions to facilitate your triumph over cravings and attainment of your objectives.

Recognize and Resolve Root Causes: Cravings may occasionally stem from underlying factors such as anxiety, depression, or trauma. If you harbor suspicions regarding this possibility, it would be advisable to actively seek the assistance of a qualified professional in order to address these concerns forthrightly and delve deeply into the underlying causes of your cravings.

Maintain a Food and Mood Journal: Maintaining a record of your dietary consumption and emotional state can facilitate the identification of patterns and causes for your cravings. This can be advantageous in formulating a strategy to surmount these challenges.

Identify Wholesome Strategies to Manage Stress: The experience of stress often leads to the emergence of cravings. Adopting wholesome methods of dealing with stress, such as engaging in physical activity, practicing mindful breathing techniques, or indulging in a soothing bath, can effectively mitigate stress levels and inhibit the emergence of cravings.

Employing constructive internal dialogue: Harnessing the power of affirming self-talk can prove instrumental in surmounting urges and cravings. Substitute pessimistic thoughts with optimistic ones, such as "I possess the ability to succeed" or "I am resilient and competent."

Establish Attainable Objectives: By establishing objectives that are within reach, one can alleviate sentiments of failure and disheartenment. Divide your objectives into more manageable, attainable tasks and commemorate each triumph along your journey.

Engage in Self-Care: Engaging in self-care activities can effectively mitigate stress and enhance overall well-being, consequently resulting in diminished cravings. Allocate time for engaging in activities that bring you pleasure and regard the practice of self-care as a priority in your daily schedule.

Exercise Portion Control: When succumbing to cravings, exercise conscious portion control. Indulge in a modest portion of your preferred culinary delight, taking delight in every morsel or sip.

Maintain Accountability: Disclose your objectives to a confidant or relative, and request their backing and responsibility. This can assist in maintaining focus and fostering motivation.

Please be advised that the process of conquering desires is a gradual one and may necessitate a substantial investment of both time and effort. Exercising patience, perseverance, and self-compassion throughout the journey holds great significance. By utilizing appropriate resources and receiving adequate assistance, you are capable of conquering cravings and attaining your objectives pertaining to health and wellness.

2

Mental Preparation

Initiating the path towards discontinuing the habit of smoking involves more than just a physical battle; it requires a mental fortitude and preparedness that drives a profound transformation. The foundation of a successful cessation journey lies in the cultivation of proper mental readiness. Within the confines of this article, we explore the significance attributed to mental preparedness, methods for cultivating the optimal mentality, and the pivotal function of resolve in surmounting the challenges associated with smoking cessation.

Appreciating the Significance of a Mental Outlook

The significance of attitude should not be underestimated. Adopting a constructive and driven attitude towards the task of smoking cessation significantly heightens the chances of achieving favorable outcomes. The process does not solely involve the cessation of a habit; rather, it encompasses the restoration of authority over one's life and well-being.

Setting Clear Intentions

Prior to making a significant commitment, it is of paramount importance to establish distinct objectives. What is the rationale behind your desire to cease the habit of smoking? What are your motivations? Enhancing your well-being, serving as a role model for those you care about, or reclaiming your autonomy, comprehending your motivations enhances your determination.

Visualizing Success

Visual representation serves as an indispensable tool in mental readiness. Devote your time to visualizing a version of yourself devoid of any smoking habits - engaging in unhindered breathing, experiencing heightened vitality, and possessing a renewed sense of vigor.

Developing a comprehensive cognitive representation of success serves to fortify your resolve and provides a valuable anchor amidst adversarial circumstances.

Positive Affirmations

Affirmations are constructive declarations that have the potential to shape one's cognitive processes. By consistently reiterating positive statements such as "I possess the ability to exercise control over my decisions" or "I possess the capacity to conquer urges," you foster a belief in your innate capability to cease harmful behaviors. These affirmations serve as a protective shield against feelings of self-doubt and the detrimental habit of engaging in negative self-talk.

Building a Support System

Psychological preparedness involves acknowledging that you need not navigate this path unaided. Seek assistance from acquaintances, close relatives, or communal organizations. Enhancing one's mental fortitude can be achieved by immersing oneself in a supportive network of individuals who have faith in one's ability to overcome obstacles and offer upliftment.

Developing Coping Strategies

Ceasing cigarette consumption frequently accompanies challenges, such as experiencing cravings and being susceptible to triggers. Having a stockpile of effective coping mechanisms is necessary for being mentally prepared. Engaging in techniques such as controlled breathing, partaking in activities of personal interest, or fostering mindfulness can provide effective means to withstand challenging circumstances without relying on smoking.

The Role of Determination

Determination lies at the core of mental readiness. It represents the resolute commitment to your choice to abstain from smoking. Foster determination by consistently reminding yourself of your underlying reasons and the favorable outcomes you strive to achieve. When confronted with obstacles, draw upon your wellspring of resolve to persevere steadfastly.

Mental readiness is the fundamental element of a triumphant endeavor to cease smoking. It revolves around harnessing the potential of one's attitude, formulating definite objectives, and acquiring effective coping mechanisms.

Please be mindful that ceasing the act of smoking entails more than simply abandoning a habit. It is, in fact, an impactful process of personal evolution, necessitating resilience of the mind, unwavering determination, and the conviction that you possess the capability to conquer challenges. Whilst traversing this path, please acknowledge that the power of your cognition serves as your most formidable companion, effectively clearing the path towards a salubrious and smokeless destiny.

Adopting a New Perspective to Achieve Success

Altering your perspective is an imperative stride towards ceasing smoking. The ability to liberate oneself from the shackles of nicotine necessitates a cognitive readjustment characterized by resolute determination, unwavering perseverance, and an optimistic perspective. This article endeavors to explore the art of altering one's mindset and the advantage of setting specific cessation objectives as a means to pave the way for a gratifying smoke-free lifestyle.

Further consequences of smoking

By now, it will have become evident to you that the cigarette serves as a manifestation of a pattern of thoughts, emotions, and behaviors. The primary factor contributing to the state of addiction to smoking can be attributed to individuals possessing a diminished sense of vitality and a lack of self-awareness. You exhibit a lack of agency in managing your own life, as evidenced by the way you succumb to the act of folding over your cigarette. Smoking is a customary practice that serves the purpose of establishing the passing of each day. The ceremony functions as a guiding force, indicating that we have made some progress over the previous day. Consider occasions such as birthdays, holidays, formal meals, casual gatherings, and other instances dictated by societal norms; all of these collectively comprise various ceremonial practices. If one adheres to them, everything proceeds favorably; however, deviating from them yields unfavorableoutcomes. This is the established modus operandi of our organization. Rituals contribute to the construction of significance, akin to how the act of smoking deceives one into perceiving progress. Allen Carr, widely renowned on a global scale for his book entitled "È facile smettere di fumare se sai come farlo"[4], understandably employs the metaphorical representation of the treadmill. Smoking affords the perception of progress while maintaining a state of immobility. It resembles the act of preparing one's suitcases for a journey, despite remaining confined within the premises of one's residence. The voyage persists within the mind, while one remains confined as a captive.

I wish to refrain from initiating unsubstantiated concerns or assigning culpability, yet I also urge you to assess previously undisclosed elements, so as to earnestly contemplate the ramifications of smoking on both your own life and those in your immediate vicinity. Cigarettes may serve as a precursor to the initiation of substance abuse, such as consumption of marijuana, alcohol, and even highly detrimental substances like cocaine and heroin. While smoking poses inherent dangers, it is imperative to exercise caution and acknowledge the evidence provided by statistics. Individuals who partake in substance abuse and engage in the consumption of drugs, alcohol, and tobacco. Have you encountered individuals with alcohol dependency who abstain from smoking? An individual who is addicted to narcotics but does not engage in smoking? Based on a study carried out by the ASL of Milan 3 in 2006, it was found that an overwhelming majority of 95% of individuals addicted to drugs engage in smoking behavior [5]. One should additionally take into account the prevailing social context, as individuals who smoke often tend to possess a diminished sense of self-worth, seek out social connections, and form a close-knit circle of like-minded individuals, thus perpetuating a harmful cycle. I have apprehensions regarding the well-being of the younger generation. Teenagers elicit a plea for assistance by means of smoking cigarettes. They desire to convey a message to individuals of a more mature age group. It signifies: "My living conditions are unfavorable and I am experiencing discomfort." Parents should be mindful of their children's distress: smoking serves as one of the most perceptible indicators. The instance commences with mature individuals, parental figures, and individuals who hold significant influence in society. If you hold positions such as executives, physicians, government officials, prominent individuals in the entertainment industry, or individuals widely admired and revered as leaders, it is strongly advised that you abstain from smoking.

Adults bear the responsibility for the well-being and guidance of young individuals. Learning is established through firsthand encounters, but most importantly, it relies on the impactful influence of the surrounding environment and the exemplification of appropriate conduct. Based on recent neurological research, it has been established that the process of learning occurs through imitation. Therefore, the previous notion of "comply with my instructions but not my actions" is no longer applicable.

Furthermore, one must consider the adverse consequences that extend beyond societal frameworks, namely the detrimental impacts on both the overall quality of life and the environment. Each passing day, the environment endures immeasurable harm as a consequence of discarded cigarette butts littered on streets, beaches, and in forested areas. It transcends the realm of mere decorum; it pertains to the preservation of our welfare through the conservation of our living environment. The "stubs" have a detrimental impact on the environment akin to that of industrial waste. City manholes get clogged. Beaches serve as the largest receptacles for discarded cigarette butts on the planet. Vast stretches of woodland vanish to accommodate expansive tobacco plantations, while other forested areas succumb to devastating blazes ignited by seemingly innocuous cigarettes. In addition to the aforementioned adverse health and societal consequences associated with addiction, it is imperative to acknowledge the multifaceted repercussions encompassing financial destitution, labor exploitation, criminal activities, and illicit trade that are intricately linked to the manufacturing and distribution of tobacco products. These are all facets that we cannot overlook.

Smoking's Endgame

I had one paternal grandfather who achieved the venerable age of 100, while my other paternal grandfather remained unknown to me. I experienced the loss of one grandmother while I was an infant, and my other grandmother was gracefully dancing at my 40th birthday celebration. Can you ascertain the individuals who engaged in smoking? I could provide numerous anecdotes pertaining to individuals who tragically lost their lives prematurely as a result of smoking, although the most poignant one that readily comes to mind is the narrative surrounding my dear friend, Johnny.

During the initial years of my third decade, an opportunity arose for employment in the construction field at a gold mining operation located in

Mauritania, a nation situated in West Africa. During this phase of my professional journey, I held the position of a Health and Safety Officer. Evidently, they sought a proficient individual with expertise in safety management for this particular project, to effectively address a complex situation. After organizing my paperwork, I subsequently arrived a few weeks later. The Sahara desert was intended to become my future place of residence. The temperature registered at 45 degrees Celsius upon my disembarkation from the aircraft. What a startling revelation. It constituted a significant transition from the frigid temperatures of -10 degrees experienced in the Sakhalin Islands of North Russia. After a rapid and lengthy conveyance lasting four hours, I reached the mine upon departing from the airport in Mauritania. The conditions were thoroughly unpleasant, characterized by scorching heat, swirling dust, and ubiquitous sand particles. Upon my arrival at the entrance, I was cordially greeted by Gerry. Initially, I failed to discern his identity due to the fact that he had donned a head covering that shielded his face and mouth from the environmental conditions. He held the position of chief safety officer for this project and was the individual who requested my presence. I have had the privilege of collaborating with Gerry in challenging construction environments, where we demonstrated excellent teamwork.

Shortly after my arrival, I found myself in Gerry's office, engaging in a discussion concerning the matters that lay before me. The site sketch was unfurled onto the desk, and the boundaries of my assigned area were delineated. Typically, the primary concerns of an individual in my current role would pertain to the ongoing tasks performed at the construction site, the responsible parties involved in the execution of these tasks, and the precise methodologies employed to ensure the safety of such operations. In addition to the aforementioned reasons, it is crucial to address the pressing security issues arising from the conflicts occurring in Mali and Libya during that period. Such discourse was absent. The sole topic of conversation pertained to the construction manager overseeing the operations within my designated vicinity. The individual in question was known as Johnny (I shall refrain from disclosing his surname) - an elder Scottish gentleman who had little regard for adhering to appropriate operational protocols or the presence of safety officers, for that matter. Gerry devoted a considerable amount of time regaling me with anecdotes detailing his team's challenges and encounters with Johnny. They were nothing short of entertaining, if I may be so bold as to say. I chuckled appreciatively at the clever maneuvers exhibited by this individual. John could not be transferred to a different position due to his strong rapport with the client. Consequently, it became incumbent upon me to supervise him closely, aiming to ensure that his actions did not jeopardize the safety of himself or others involved in the project. Alright," I replied, "let us explore the possibilities and evaluate what actions I can undertake. I was provided with a pickup truck, as well as all the necessary equipment to ensure my survival within a desert setting. Subsequently, I proceeded towards the designated location of my employment.

My intention was to encounter this individual named Johnny, establish a connection with him, and subsequently develop the rapport between us. The approach involving incentives or rewards tends to be the most convenient, though not consistently the most efficacious, particularly within the construction industry. However, this was the original intention. Upon my arrival at the compound, I observed a configuration comprised of numerous 40-foot shipping containers, purpose-built workshops, and modular office units. I discovered a modest area in which to establish my business, and subsequently embarked upon my undertaking. I encountered several individuals from the region, and despite my modest proficiency in French, I discerned that the primary operational region lay along a pipeline connecting the power generation facility and the crushing facility. I presumed that Johnny would be in that vicinity, therefore I proceeded to embark upon the direction by boarding the truck.

Observing the individuals toiling amidst extreme temperatures, I expressed gratitude for the fortunate circumstances that exempted me from such laborious conditions. In the past, I had completed all of those tasks, and now it was my responsibility to rotate in the large American truck and monitor the proceedings. I had acquired my position through merit, commencing from an entry-level role, and never received any undue advantages in my endeavors within the construction field. I encountered a collective of individuals diligently engaged in the task of maintaining a specific segment of the 20-inch pipeline. I observed Johnny amidst the group. I immediately recognized him; for who else but him would don a pair of crimson footwear? I parked the vehicle, equipped myself with a helmet, and proceeded to approach him on foot. I gradually descended into the granular terrain, where even traversing this location proved to be an arduous ordeal. He observed my approach and proceeded to distance himself from my presence. What was he doing? I thought to myself. Typically, in such circumstances, it is customary for the gentleman to extend his greetings, excluding Johnny. He engaged in a distinct style of play. Well, I am equally capable of engaging in that same activity. At any rate, I ultimately managed to catch up with him. "You're Johnny", I said. "Could you elaborate on the basis of your statement?" he promptly responded. I remarked, "It appears quite unorthodox for anyone else to be donning crimson footwear amidst a construction site," as my gaze fixated on his Elvis-inspired shoes. The situation became more intense when I inadvertently stepped on his impeccably crafted red footwear in order to verify the validity of his assertion that they were equipped with steel toe caps. Johnny was older than me by a margin of at least 30 years, yet his behavior did not reflect his age. I must assert that he was a resilient Scottish lad. Each chest had risen, and the escalating verbal confrontation was on the verge of becoming physical when several nearby American individuals intervened. A confrontation ensued between myself and Johnny. He possessed strong roots and extensive familiarity with the landscape and the laborers, whereas I lacked mobility and progress.

We experienced numerous encounters and conflicts during the initial weeks, but a pivotal event transpired on the premises that completely altered the course of events. We were compelled to collaborate in order to manage a conflagration in one of the warehouses housing items of great value. We deployed a team on both sides of the structure in order to effectively manage the fire, and ultimately succeeded in extinguishing it without causing any harm to the valuable equipment present. We emerged from that experience with a significantly higher level of mutual respect. Subsequently, we developed an amicable rapport and transitioned into a collaborative partnership rather than engaging in adversarial interactions. I collaborated with Johnny for a durationof two years on that particular project, and truthfully, I have never experienced such a high level of enjoyment or mirth in any professional undertaking prior, regardless of the challenges encountered. This can be attributed to Johnny's inclination towards Scottish humor and wit. We shared numerous commonalities and developed a strong friendship. Surprisingly enough, he eventually proved to be more favorable than initially anticipated and emerged as my most fervent proponent of Safety. It transpired that he was strongly committed to ensuring safety, yet he displayed resistance towards receiving instructions and adhering to authoritative directives regarding proper conduct.

Regrettably, Johnny's state of health was subpar. His countenance bore the signs of a life marred by the consequences of detrimental health decisions, unmistakably indicating his compromised state of well-being. He exhibited a slight limp and occasionally emitted a cough every 4 or 5 strides in order to alleviate congestion in his throat. He informed me that he had experienced a cardiac episode during his previous employment and dedicated a significant amount of time to recuperation. Based on my observations, he had not made any lifestyle modifications to enhance his overall well-being. He habitually indulged in heavy smoking and consumed alcohol whenever circumstances allowed. We would indulge in laughter over an amusing remark, while Johnny would invariably experience the onset of choking and gasping for breath. I frequently expressed concern and inquired about his well-being. I pondered the remaining duration of old Johnny. Indeed, Johnny was not of advanced age. Despite being in his sixth decade of life, his appearance did not reflect his age. In my office, there was a defibrillator named Johnny 1, and I possessed another one in my vehicle referred to as Johnny 2. Frequent humorous exchanges regarding the subject transpired between us, albeit deep down, I held a nagging suspicion that I would eventually be compelled to utilize them on his behalf, despite my fervent desires and supplications pleading against such eventuality.

Upon returning from a two-week period of authorized absence, I was informed that Johnny had experienced a medical emergency at the premises several days prior, necessitating immediate transportation to a hospital located in a city approximately four hours away. There was limited information available regarding Johnny's condition, with the prevailing sentiment being that the situation was dire. I made attempts to obtain information from the hospital, yet they maintained their silence, notwithstanding my amiable demeanor during our phone conversation. Similar to the rest of the individuals, I, too, was obliged to endure a period of anticipation as the hospital deliberated upon disseminating information to us. After a span of multiple days, I received a telephone call, wherein the caller happened to be Johnny. "Johnny, may I inquire about your well-being?" I questioned with a sense of eagerness. I failed to identify the gentleman on the opposite side. The individual I encountered was a departure from the familiar Johnny I knew - a resilient individual who displayed a sense of apathy and disinterest towards any concerns or worries. This individual exhibited an absence of vitality and was consumed by apprehension. He expressed his distress with tears running down his face, conveying his profound concern about the imminent loss of his lower limbs. He was devoid of any companionship or familial support during his hospitalization. Shortly after our dialogue commenced, he abruptly terminated the call or disconnected, presumably to spare me from witnessing his distressed state. Despite exerting diligent effort, no further communication was received from Johnny. After the passage of a few days, we received information indicating that Johnny had succumbed while undergoing a surgical procedure. That period was characterized by sorrow on the premises, as Johnny's positive influence extended beyond my own experience. Even now, I find myself ponder upon Johnny and the many enjoyable moments we shared; it is disheartening to reflect upon the untimely demise of such an exceptional individual and the potential left unrealized. There may be those who assign fault to the hospital for negligence, but I would contend that Johnny's unfortunate demise can be attributed to his own imprudent choices, with smoking emerging as the primary factor. I had not yet quit smoking at that point; however, I can assure you that I was aware of the necessity to stop. If I were not to derive invaluable lessons from this encounter, one's mental stability would undoubtedly come under scrutiny.

We are all acquainted with individuals dear to us who have prematurely departed from this world as a result of tobacco use. It is an undeniable reality that persisting in this habit will inevitably lead us down a similar path of untimely demise, regardless of our resilience. Allow me to present a sobering perspective, as there is no intention to instill fear but rather convey the unvarnished reality. One may contemplate the future and state, "I shall relinquish smoking at a later juncture when circumstances allow," however, this notion only resides in a realm of fantasy and serves as a flimsy pretext to defer the necessary action. Each cigarette consumed contributes to an incremental decline in your physical strength, while simultaneously augmenting the sway that they possess over you. At present, it is imperative to initiate proactive measures. Be getting ready.

Prescription Medications

Smoking is a prevalent addiction with significant global implications, capturing the lives of millions across the globe. Cessation of tobacco use can be a challenging endeavor owing to the powerful grip nicotine has both on the body and the mind. Fortunately, there exists a multitude of approaches and techniques, including pharmaceutical interventions, that can aid individuals in overcoming this addiction. This article aims to explore the process of selecting the most suitable prescription medication and its significant role in aiding smoking cessation.

The cessation of smoking is not applicable to all individuals universally. Due to the distinct experiences of each individual, what may prove effective for one person might not yield the same results for another. Given their intended purpose of reducing both nicotine cravings and withdrawal symptoms, it can be concluded that prescription medications can be highly advantageous during this transitional phase. Presented below are several pharmacological options frequently prescribed for smoking cessation:

Nicotine Replacement Therapy (NRT): NRT encompasses the practice of utilizing nicotine substitutes, such as gum, patches, inhalers, and lozenges, readily available for purchase without the need for a prescription or over-the-counter. In order to aid in managing withdrawal symptoms, they furnish a regulated quantity of nicotine at a reduced level. It is advisable to seek counsel from your healthcare professional regarding the appropriate NRT product and dosage.

Bupropion (Zyban): The atypical antidepressant bupropion, commonly referred to as Zyban, has demonstrated efficacy as an aid in smoking cessation. In order to mitigate nicotine cravings, it modifies brain chemistry. It is imperative that only under the guidance of medical professionals should this substance be administered, and its availability is restricted exclusively through a prescribed course of action.

Varenicline (Chantix): Varenicline (Chantix) is a pharmaceutical medication designed with the primary objective of aiding individuals in their smoking cessation efforts. It operates by targeting nicotine receptors within the brain, thereby mitigating manifestations of withdrawal while concurrently reducing the inclination towards smoking. It is imperative to adhere to the prescribed dosage as directed by a healthcare provider, similar to the manner in which other prescribed medications are to be taken.

The optimal pharmaceutical treatment for you will be contingent upon various factors, encompassing your medical background, current state of health, and personal preferences. Please adhere to these procedures in order to make an informed decision:

Seek Medical Guidance: To initiate the process of choosing a prescribed medication for smoking cessation, it is advisable to engage in a discussion with a healthcare practitioner. They are likely to assess your overall health status, engage in a discussion regarding your smoking behavior, and recommend the most optimal treatment approach.

Account for Potential Consequences: Each medication carries the risk of adverse effects. For example, individuals who utilize Chantix may potentially cite experiencing insomnia or highly vivid nightmares, whereas those employing NRT may encounter sensations of heightened oral dryness. It is of utmost importance to thoroughly discuss these potential side effects with your physician and carefully weigh them against the benefits of smoking cessation.

Examine Medical Background: The selection of a medication necessitates an evaluation of your medical background. If individuals possess specific preexisting medical conditions, they might not be suitable candidates for certain pharmaceutical substances. Exercise caution in providing comprehensive details regarding your medical history to your healthcare practitioner.

Establish a Target Cessation Date: Regardless of the substance of choice, it is imperative to designate a specific date for cessation. It provides individuals with a defined objective to strive for, fostering a state of mental readiness in anticipation of the journey.

Integrate Medication with Support: The optimum approach entails combining counseling or behavioral treatment with the administration of prescription drugs. A considerable number of individuals perceive value in embracing the services of a therapist or enrolling in a smoking cessation program as a means to effectively confront the psychological aspects intrinsic to addiction.

Obstacles Encountered During The Cessation Of Smoking

Ceasing the habit of smoking is a praiseworthy undertaking, yet it is often accompanied by a myriad of obstacles that individuals commonly face throughout their journey. Acknowledging and anticipating these difficulties can assist individuals who smoke in effectively navigating the journey towards achieving a smoke-free lifestyle. The following are several prevalent obstacles encountered when attempting to quit the habit of smoking:

1. Nicotine Withdrawal: Nicotine, the substance responsible for addiction in tobacco products, induces a state of physical dependence. During the process of relinquishing smoking, individuals may encounter withdrawal symptoms,

encompassing but not limited to irritability, anxiety, depression, impaired cognitive function, agitation, and strong urges for nicotine. These symptoms can present significant challenges during the cessation process and have the potential to result in relapse if not effectively addressed.

2. Psychological Dependence: Alongside the physical dependency, smoking frequently becomes entwined with individuals' daily routines, habits, and emotional coping mechanisms. Overcoming these psychological connections can pose a considerable obstacle. Individuals who engage in smoking might encounter stimuli in specific circumstances or emotional states, including stress, social interactions, or post-meal periods, that can exacerbate cravings and pose

challenges in resisting the inclination to smoke.

3. Social Conformity: Smoking is frequently a communal practice, and abstaining from it may occasionally engender sentiments of seclusion or marginalization. The influence exerted by one's peers or close relatives who persist in smoking can present an additional obstacle. Moreover, environments characterized by widespread smoking, such as bars or social gatherings, may pose a potential risk for individuals to revert to their previous smoking habits.

4. Insufficient Assistance: Establishing a robust network of support is imperative when endeavoring to cease smoking. Nevertheless, certain individuals might find themselves lacking the essential assistance from their acquaintances,

relatives, or colleagues, thereby rendering the endeavor more arduous. Lack of motivation and accountability could pose a greater challenge in sustaining one's efforts to quit without adequate support and comprehension.

5. Undesirable Weight Increase: A common concern among individuals upon smoking cessation pertains to the potential for weight gain, as nicotine has the ability to subdue appetite and enhance metabolic functions. Certain individuals seek solace in food as a surrogate for cigarettes, resulting in an increase in body weight. Attaining weight management while undergoing smoking cessation necessitates the adoption of nutritious dietary practices and sustained participation in consistent physical exercise.

6. Reversion: The act of quitting smoking seldom follows a straightforward trajectory. Instances of relapse may manifest, even subsequent to the initial attainment of success. One minor mistake can potentially result in a complete regression if not effectively addressed. It is imperative to regard relapses as opportunities for growth rather than shortcomings, and to devise tactics to proactively manage and handle potential setbacks.

The prospect of overcoming these challenges might appear formidable; however, it is crucial to bear in mind that numerous individuals have managed to effectively cease tobacco consumption in spite of these impediments. By adopting the appropriate mindset, receiving adequate support, and implementing effective strategies, individuals can surmount these obstacles and progress towards a more salubrious existence devoid of smoking.

Exploring Health-conscious Options: Transforming Your Way of Life

Integrating Physical Activity to Reduce Urge for Unhealthy Food

Physical activity serves as a powerful asset in your endeavor to cease smoking, not solely due to its myriad health advantages but also because it effectively reduces cravings and bolsters your overall state of being. Through the adoption of a consistent exercise regimen, individuals are arming themselves with a potent instrument that not only aids in controlling cravings, but also strengthens their dedication to a tobacco-free existence.

Understanding the Connection:

Neurological Implications: Physical exercise promotes the secretion of endorphins, acting as natural mood-elevating agents. These chemicals elicit favorable emotions and aid in alleviating the distress caused by cravings.

Mitigation of Stress: Engaging in physical activities mitigates stress and anxiety, both of which can serve as catalysts for cravings. As stress decreases, so too does the inclination to engage in smoking behavior.

- Redirection of focus: Participating in physical activity serves as a beneficial redirection of attention away from cravings. The emphasis placed on bodily motion and sensory perception diverts your attention from the inclination to engage in smoking.

Effective Exercise Strategies:

1. Cardiovascular Exercises: Physical activities such as running, biking, swimming, and engaging in dance movements have the ability to elevate heart rate, enhance blood circulation, and stimulate the secretion of endorphins.

2. Integrating Resistance Training: Implement resistance training routines that encompass the use of weights, resistance bands, or the individual's own body weight. Enhancing metabolic function and promoting overall physical fitness are associated with the development of muscle mass.

- Yoga and Pilates: These disciplines incorporate bodily movements along with mindfulness techniques, fostering a sense of tranquility and self-consciousness, while simultaneously enhancing flexibility and muscularity.

4. Interval Training: Engage in alternating periods of vigorous intensity and periods of lower-intensity recovery. Interval training provides a time-effective means of attaining cardiovascular advantages.

5. Collective Exercises: Participating in collective physical fitness sessions or group sports activities introduces a social aspect, fostering a sense of camaraderie and responsibility.

Creating an Exercise Routine:

1. Opt for Pleasurable Activities: Opt for exercises that you find enjoyable to enhance the probability of adhering to your fitness regimen. The greater your anticipation of your exercise sessions,

the higher likelihood of maintaining a regular routine.

2. Establish Attainable Objectives: Begin by setting feasible goals that progressively escalate in both intensity and duration. Maintaining a consistent approach is of utmost importance; even brief sessions can yield advantageous outcomes.

3. Introduce Diversity: Alternate between diverse forms of exercises to avoid monotony and activate different muscle groups.

4. Maintain a Consistent Schedule: Develop a regular exercise routine that harmonizes with your daily activities. Maintaining a consistent approach amplifies the beneficial impacts on cravings and mood.

Maximizing the Benefits:

Mitigate the occurrence of relapses: By actively participating in physical exercise, individuals can effectively decrease the probability of relapsing by providing a wholesome means of addressing stress and cravings.

Mind-Body Connection: Utilize physical activity as an opportunity to engage in mindful practice. Direct your focus to your breath, sensations, and movements, fostering a robust union between your mind and body.

Grant Yourself a Reward: Commemorate milestones attained throughout your fitness journey. Indulge in the purchase of a fresh exercise ensemble, partake in a therapeutic massage, or choose another avenue of self-pampering.

Embrace the Potential of Mobility

Integrating physical activity into your daily routine not only bolsters your physical well-being, but also exerts a profound influence on your mental and emotional welfare. Through the reduction of cravings, alleviation of stress, and improvement of one's overall mood, engaging in physical activity becomes an organic supplement to your endeavor of ceasing tobacco consumption. As you embrace the efficacy of physical activity, you are actively forging a future characterized by enhanced well-being and dynamism—one stride, one exercise routine, and one tobacco-free day at a time.

Maximizing Nutritional Requirements for Rehabilitation and Purification

The selection of a well-balanced diet plays a fundamental role in your recuperation and purification process subsequent to your cessation of smoking. Through the provision of appropriate nutrients, one fosters the inherent capacities of the body to undergo healing, restoration, and rejuvenation. Deliberately choosing nourishing foods that support detoxification and improve your overall state of health can expedite your journey towards a smoke-free existence characterized by energy and vitality.

Comprehending the Importance of Nutrition:

Detoxifying the Body: Ceasing the habit of smoking initiates a inherent process of eliminating toxins. Adequate nourishment facilitates the enhanced efficiency of your body in eliminating accumulated toxins.

Cellular Regeneration: Consumption of nourishing foods delivers the essential components necessary for cellular repair, fostering general well-being.

Enhancing Energy Levels: Consuming a well-balanced diet provides the necessary fuel for your body's sustenance, enabling you to remain dynamically engaged and attentive throughout your cessation voyage.

Now, we shall proceed to the principle:

In order to permanently cease smoking, it is imperative to adhere to a singular, uncomplicated guideline: abstain from partaking in a solitary cigarette during the designated timeframe of three consecutive days. I reiterate the request that you abstain from smoking a cigarette during that specific time period for the consecutive three days.

For instance, in the case of Days 1-3, if you typically have your initial cigarette at 7 am, I would advise you to refrain from smoking it until the same time on Day 1. Instead, I would recommend waiting until the time of your second cigarette, which, in this illustration, would be 8 am, and consuming it then. Likewise, you should proceed through the remainder of the day by adhering to the specific timings for the remaining 9 cigarettes. Did you get it?

For Days 4-6, it is advisable to adhere to the aforementioned straightforward guideline: refrain from smoking one cigarette at a specific time. Begin by abstaining from your second cigarette at 8 am, and patiently abstain until the designated time for your third cigarette, which in this example would be 10 am. From 10 am onwards, resume smoking and proceed to consume the remaining eight cigarettes for that day according to their respective scheduled times.

Furthermore, it should be observed that by the present time, which is the sixth day, one should be able to refrain from smoking for a minimum of 2 to 3 hours after awakening. This accomplishment stands as a significant milestone for numerous individuals who have been habitual smokers.

In accordance with this illustration, the individual who engages in smoking at 7 am presently has the potential to abstain from smoking for a duration of three hours until 10 am. Certain individuals may inquire as to what is the significance of this matter. As illustrated in previous chapters regarding the concept of chemical gradients, we are gradually reducing the quantity of chemical intake within our bodies by 10% on a tripartite basis. This method is employed to train our bodies to tolerate the deprivation of these chemicals, thus mitigating perpetual cravings for them. Furthermore, any tasks that require your attention during the period from 7 am to 10 am should be diligently pursued.

In the event that there is an occasion affiliated with those cigarettes during the period of abstinence, you must seek an alternative means to attain that occasion. As an illustration, in my particular scenario, I am compelled to engage in the act of elimination. Consequently, I indulged in my inaugural cigarette before 7 am. Therefore, as a viable alternative, I have adopted a newly formed beneficial practice of consuming a significant quantity of fruits during the evening meal from the preceding day, thereby facilitating improved bowel movements the following morning.

Now, Returning to the methodology, during Days 7-9, you will discontinue the consumption of the third cigarette at this point, specifically at 10 am, and refrain from smoking until 11.30 am. Subsequently, you may proceed to smoke the remaining seven cigarettes of the day at their designated time slots.

On Days 10-12, you cease consumption of the fourth cigarette. This cessation occurs at 11.30 am, and you abstain from smoking until 1 pm, at which point you proceed to smoke the remaining six cigarettes of the day according to their respective schedules.

From Days 13-15, you abstain from the 5th cigarette, specifically the one consumed at 1 pm, while adhering to the scheduled consumption of the remaining 5 cigarettes throughout the day.

By the 15th day, you would come to the realization that your body has the capability to endure half of the day without any dependence on smoking a single cigarette. Due to the gradual reduction of chemical intake every 3 days. By now, you would have ceased the consumption of 50% of the chemicals you previously ingested 15 days ago.

In my particular circumstances, I achieved a state where I became capable of enduring the entire duration from morning to evening, until 4 pm, without the necessity or inclination to engage in the act of smoking a cigarette, and this was achieved entirely devoid of any cravings. At that moment, I attained a deep comprehension that this methodology is yielding remarkable results, enabling me to renounce the habit of smoking and embrace a life devoid of tobacco dependency and yearning for cigarettes.

In this manner, you progressively reduce your cigarette consumption by quitting one cigarette every three days. By the 16th to 18th day, you cease smoking the sixth cigarette at precisely 3 pm.

Between the nineteenth and twenty-first days, cessation occurred on the seventh day at 4 pm.

During the period encompassing days 22-24, you terminated your eighth activity at a time of 5.30 pm.

On the 25th to the 27th of the month, you successfully abstained from smoking, with the 9th and second-to-last cigarette being foregoing at 6.30 pm.

On the 28th day, you discontinued the final cigarette, which was the tenth, at precisely 8.30 pm. Do not excessively prolong the usage of the final cigarette, nor should any sentiment be bestowed upon it. You regard it on par with the others, with equal standard and regularity.

Here is your schedule for the end of the workday.

Cigarette 1: 7 am, Abstain from Tobacco Use from the Onset till Day 1-3

Cigarette 2: 8 am, Abstain from Smoking Starting on Day 4-6

Cigarette 3: 10 am, Abstain from this starting from Day 7-9

Cigarette number four was smoked at 11:30 am and was discontinued from day ten to day twelve.

Cigarette 5: 1 pm, Abstain from Smoking from Days 13 to 15.

Cigarette number 6: At 3 pm, cease this habit from the 16th to the 18th day.

Cigarette Number 7: 4 pm, Abstain From This Habit Between Days 19-21

Cigarette 8: 5.30 pm, Discontinue usage from Day 22-24

Cigarette nine: commencing at 6:30 in the evening, abstain from this habit between days 25 and 27.

Smoking Session 10: At 8:30 pm, Discontinue this habit on the 28th day.

Therefore, if you are a moderate smoker with a daily consumption of 10 cigarettes, adhering to this approach will result in a complete cessation of the habit within a span of 28 days. Starting on day 28, you will transition into a smoke-free lifestyle indefinitely.

If you happen to be a moderate smoker who consistently consumes 20 cigarettes on a daily basis, it will require a period of approximately 58 days for you to successfully abstain from smoking.

I meticulously adhered to this specific technique 16 years ago, wherein I progressively reduced my consumption of cigarettes by quitting one every 3 days. By doing so, I effectively trained my body to endure the presence of Nicotine and the numerous other addictive chemicals found in cigarettes, systematically reducing their intake by 10% every 3 days, 30% from the 7th day, 50% from the 13th day, 80% from the 22nd day, and completely abstaining from them in a span of 28 days.

As of the 28th day, I successfully abstained from smoking.

Attitude to embrace throughout this endeavor: Remain calm, maintain a sense of normalcy, and continue with your daily routines. Please remain cognizant of the designated time for your next cigarette and engage in positive self-dialogue in the event of a craving.

Significance of Commemoration: As you engage in celebrations, your nervous system acknowledges their positive effects and actively endeavors to facilitate their recurrence. Therefore, commemorate each and every one of your triumphs every three days when you forgo that one cigarette at that particular moment. One has the option of offering oneself praise and encouragement, partaking in a favored meal, or sharing the progress achieved with one's family, loved ones, or acquaintances. Please ensure you remember and promptly engage in the act of celebration.

Strategies for occupying oneself during the period of abstinence:

During the interim period before your next cigarette, I kindly request that you adhere to specific directives.

First and foremost, I would like to urge you to consistently consume ample amounts of water during the intervals wherein you refrain from smoking. As an illustration, if you refrain from smoking between the hours of 7:00 AM to 10:00 AM, I kindly request that during this duration you consume a significant amount of water. It attenuates the chemical components within the cigarette that have permeated to the cellular level, thereby dampening the craving.

The efficacy of self-dialogue: Additionally, should you experience any inclinations during the course of this endeavor, engage in the practice of self-communication. Self-dialogue involves the act of conversing with oneself and issuing instructions or directives to oneself in response to specific circumstances.

As an illustration, consider engaging in self-dialogue and enunciating the following statement aloud: "I shall exclusively provide you with the cigarette at the designated time, prior to which it will not be bestowed upon you.

I reiterate, the aforementioned cigarette shall be granted solely at the specified time, prior to which it shall not be bestowed upon you, concluding the matter."

Engaging in internal dialogue can aid in maintaining focus over extended periods. If you anticipate a wait of an additional hour or half an hour, kindly articulate it as 'Not at this moment, but in precisely one hour,' and 'Not at this moment, but in exactly thirty minutes,' respectively. Through this practice, one can cultivate the ability to maintain mental fortitude. While engaging in this activity, regard your inner being with the nurturing care one would provide to a young individual.

This would prove to be highly advantageous at the commencement of your journey, as well as upon reaching the milestone of 50% progress, specifically after reducing your consumption to the point of refraining from a fifth cigarette.

In order to combat the internal dialogue that may arise, employing the practice of self-dialogue could prove beneficial. This method can be particularly effective during the early hours of the day when one's body or mind tends to engage in deceptive tactics, manifesting as a small voice posing questions such as, "Why am I unable to partake in smoking at this moment?" Why must I endure a protracted period of waiting until the afternoon or evening? Merely redirect that inner dialogue, counter the thoughts, and assert, 'I shall permit you to smoke, but only at 1 pm or 4 pm, as designated.'

It can be likened to the way parents nurture and care for their child, with the individual taking on a similar role towards themselves. As an illustration, when a child persistently requests ice cream from their mother, it is often observed that the mother may respond by stating, "You shall be granted ice cream, but only once you have completed your homework." Mother will provide you with chocolate solely on the condition that you maintain silence. Likewise, you have the ability to train your mind to exhibit patience.

Please take into consideration that an alternative approach would be to incorporate your individual intrinsic motivation factor in the internal dialogue that was discussed in 7.

Additional point: It is worth considering that the recently attached significance of smoking can also be incorporated into one's internal dialogues. We observed this phenomenon in the preceding 8.

Strategies For Achieving Long-Term Smoking Cessation.

Make the decision to cease smoking and ensure that you are fully prepared.

This marks the preliminary stage towards cessation of smoking. In this context, you are providing personal assurance that regardless of any obstacles encountered, you will not regress or retreat.

You can attain this objective through comprehensive preparation, encompassing matters such as making arrangements for necessary replacements, discerning effective and ineffective strategies, eliminating potential distractions, and refraining from consuming excessively sweet or salty foods. Such dietary choices may lead to undesirable weight gain, which can diminish your motivation to quit smoking and increase the likelihood of relapse.

Recognize and steer clear of factors that elicit a response

Discovering the underlying factors that prompt your smoking behavior will assist in ceasing this habit. What do you believe is the underlying cause of cigarette cravings? Does your occupation elicit feelings of stress, or would you benefit from engaging in more leisurely activities? What specific factors motivate you to engage in smoking? I am confident that you possess responses to these inquiries, assuming you did not bypass this section.

After determining the underlying reasons for smoking, it is important to be cognizant of the triggers that precede this behavior, specifically the specific sequence of events that culminate in the act of lighting a cigarette. For example, if your occupational timetable acts as a catalyst, ascertain the precise timeframe during which you experience the urge to engage in smoking. Subsequently, schedule a preceding recess and allocate a less demanding and enjoyable task during that designated timeframe. Establish an alarm mechanism to ensure personal responsibility and promptly disengage from the triggering stimulus as soon as the alarm is activated, irrespective of any ongoing activities.

The same principle applies to the influence exerted by friends or peer pressure. If social events tend to influence your emotional state, exercise caution and meticulously select the gatherings you participate in. There are perpetually valid justifications for abstaining from a raucous gathering, hence locate one and employ it.

Formulate a compelling rationale" or "Establish a robust foundation

This is for clarity. When one reaches a state of unequivocal understanding regarding the motivations behind cessation of smoking, one is consistently compelled to strive towards the attainment of said objective.

Each and every habit, lifestyle choice, purpose, decision-making process, and instance of attaining clarity inevitably stems from your conscious articulation of the query, "What is the underlying reason that impels me to embark upon this endeavor?" Accordingly, what serves as your driving force to cease smoking?

Please refrain from perceiving this as a mere motivational discourse; it is not. A significant number of individuals tend to undervalue the influence that seemingly insignificant aspects of life possess. Your reason for doing so is one of those commonly used and trivialized aspects. I kindly request that you relinquish that mindset and approach this matter with utmost seriousness. Regardless of your reason, it is imperative that you ensure its authenticity. Subsequently, transcribe it onto a sticky note or set it as a recurring reminder on your mobile device. Rest assured, I give you my word that it is effective, without any deception.

Notify your dear ones.

Inform your loved ones regarding your determination to cease smoking and communicate to them the ways in which they can actively contribute towards the realization of your objective. Kindly request that they hold you responsible and assure them that you will reciprocate this accountability. Ensure that all individuals are in alignment regarding the current stage of progress and the subsequent course of action.

Ideally, they will provide you with their support and prevent you from experiencing a relapse.

Ensure that you consistently acknowledge and celebrate your achievements on a daily basis.

This method happens to be among the most effective ways to cease any habit or routine; merely providing yourself with daily rewards for each incremental effort made to abstain from smoking. It will serve as an encouragement to persevere.

Are you aware of the exact amount of money expended on tobacco consumption on a daily basis? You have the option to utilize various online calculators to ascertain the precise amount of savings that would accrue upon ceasing the habit of smoking. As a token of appreciation, consider earmarking a portion of those monetary gains to indulge in a truly beneficial endeavor, such as indulging in a rejuvenating body treatment at a spa or enjoying quality time with your loved ones.

Seek a substitute for your yearnings

Ceasing the consumption of tobacco products leads to the occurrence of headaches, depletion of energy levels, and deterioration in mood due to the insufficiency of nicotine. In order to prevent or address withdrawal symptoms, it is advisable to substitute the deficiency with "nicotine therapy," comprising nicotine gum, lozenges, and patches. Rest assured, the aforementioned cessation methods are secure and reliable strategies endorsed and sanctioned by the Center for Disease Control and Prevention.

Additionally, it is possible to intermittently exert pressure on a handball when experiencing the urge, or alternatively, engage in the act of chewing menthol-infused gum to occupy the oral cavity. Occasionally, indulging in the act of mastication can aid in diverting one's desire to partake in smoking.

Alter or substitute your established practices

Altering your customary daily regimen can potentially impede your inclination to engage in smoking, as it entails modifying your energy levels, mood, and overall mental state at various intervals throughout the day. It is highly probable that the new routine will not evoke any associations with smoking.

Over the course of time, the newly established routine gradually becomes your accustomed norm. As an illustration, should you typically engage in smoking activities approximately at 8 pm, prior to retiring for the night, you may instead alter this habit by advancing your sleeping schedule or engaging in an online game that demands complete attentiveness.

Reduce your access

Exercise restraint in frequenting environments that evoke associations with smoking. To cease smoking, it is imperative to distance oneself from the company that entices and influences this behavior.

Ensure that your household is equipped with ample supplies of vegetables, fruits, grains, and proteins that offer prolonged satiation for the oral cavity. Rather than frequenting smoking areas, it would be advisable to visit locations where individuals who do not smoke tend to gather. This approach will greatly facilitate your active cessation of smoking.

Take calming exercises

Undoubtedly, one of the rationales behind your smoking habit is to alleviate stress and maintain a state of composure. However, its duration is limited. In lieu of smoking, you can engage in calming strolls and partake in the enjoyment of soothing melodies.

An alternative approach to cessation of smoking entails expressing and channeling one's emotions. Certain individuals engage in smoking as a means of alleviating the anger they experience during specific moments. Rather than engaging in smoking, opt to engage in conversation with someone during such circumstances. Engage in verbal communication, express emotions through tears, engage in laughter, practice deep diaphragmatic breathing, engage in physical activity, take a pause from tasks, reduce the pace of activities, and document your feelings through written reflection. This promotes self-control and enables the conscious prevention of smoking.

Declutter your home

After consuming your final cigarette, you have made the decision to abstain from smoking. Presently is the opportune moment to ensure that the ultimate iteration of said item serves as the conclusive final occurrence.

Dispose of any additional cigarettes present within your residence, engage in a thorough and comprehensive cleaning, launder your garments, arrange your living area systematically, and eliminate any items that could serve as reminders of smoking. This method effectively facilitates the relinquishment of any recurring behavior. Implementing a decluttering practice facilitates the mitigation of odor and, naturally, restricts the ability to engage in smoking.

2

C. Deliberation Regarding the Consequences Arising from Defective Approaches

The extensive drawbacks and shortcomings of these deficient

cessation strategies have wide-ranging and significant implications for an individual's overall welfare. Anxiety and depression are widely observed side effects that individuals commonly endure amidst the process of cessation. The dependence on self-control or the perpetual search for alternatives can engender feelings of privation and forfeiture, leading to emotional anguish and a sense of being inundated.

Excessive weight gain is a prevailing concern often linked to ineffective cessation techniques. Nicotine functions as a substance that diminishes appetite, and when individuals discontinue smoking without addressing the fundamental factors contributing to their addiction, they may resort to food as a surrogate for the oral inclination and emotional solace previously obtained from smoking. This phenomenon has the potential to contribute to an increase in body weight, compounding the difficulties faced during the cessation process and potentially impacting one's self-image and overall well-being.

Such imperfect methodologies frequently prove inadequate in offering a viable, enduring remedy, ultimately resulting in recurrence and disillusionment. The pattern of discontinuing and recommencing can be discouraging and may foster feelings of despair among individuals striving to break free from their dependence on nicotine.

Moreover, placing exclusive trust in one's determination or alternatives may perpetuate the notion that ceasing to smoke is a difficult and joyless endeavor, further cementing the belief that one must sacrifice something pleasurable. This particular way of thinking can give rise to a psychological obstacle, fostering a perpetual struggle during the cessation endeavor and consequently heightening the likelihood of regression.

The traditional methods employed for cessation of smoking and conquering nicotine dependency have notable limitations. They place their attention on the superficial indications instead of addressing the underlying factors and do not offer a comprehensive solution that addresses both the physical and psychological components of addiction.

In the subsequent chapters, we shall delve into an alternative approach that extends beyond sheer determination and replacement measures. This approach will offer a comprehensive methodology for overcoming smoking habits, enabling individuals to liberate themselves from the grip of nicotine dependence and adopt a lifestyle void of smoking, devoid of any negative impacts such as anxiety, depression, or weight gain. The forthcoming expedition might present difficulties, yet, equipped with appropriate resources and comprehension, one can surmount the obstacles and triumphantly achieve liberation.

3

The Solution Unveiled

I

In the preceding chapter, we examined the hindrances and constraints associated with conventional approaches to cessation in the realm of nicotine addiction. Now, we are poised to present a groundbreaking approach that presents a resolution—a methodology that surpasses reliance on sheer determination, alternatives, and catchy tactics. This approach endeavors to afford individuals a seamless and gratifying trajectory towards cessation, while concurrently forestalling the onset of anxiety, depression, and weight gain.

A. An Exposition of the Problem-Solving Technique

The approach advocated in this book represents a significant departure from conventional methods for quitting smoking and conquering nicotine dependence. It is not merely a simplistic remedy, but rather a comprehensive framework that tackles both the psychological and physiological aspects of addiction. By gaining a comprehensive understanding of the true essence of nicotine addiction and daring to question the fallacies it presents, you can commence a profound and life-altering expedition towards a lifestyle free from the clutches of smoking.

This approach is informed by the experiences and insights of individuals who have effectively ceased smoking through a comparable methodology. Their narratives serve as a testament to the efficacy and potency of this approach, imparting optimism and motivation for your personal endeavor.

B. Elucidation regarding the absence of necessity for willpower, substitutes, or gimmicks in this approach

An important characteristic that sets this method apart is its divergence from the conventional dependence on self-control, alternatives, or novelty factors. Rather than engaging in a struggle against cravings or substituting nicotine with alternative substances, this approach centers on altering one's perception of smoking and the use of nicotine. It equips you with the means to liberate yourself from the notion that tobacco delivers authentic enjoyment or relief, while revealing the inherent character of nicotine addiction as a ruinous and oppressive influence.

The individual is often burdened significantly when relying solely on strength of determination as the foundation for smoking cessation. The consistent challenge and opposition can give rise to sensations of deprivation and turn quitting into a perpetual struggle. This approach offers an alternative method, aiming to assist you in reevaluating your mindset and perception surrounding smoking, ultimately altering its desirability into an undesirable state. Through examining the underlying factors contributing to addiction and critically questioning the erroneous beliefs associated with smoking, one has the ability to attain emancipation from the reliance on self-control.

Alternative options such as nicotine gums, patches, or e-cigarettes may appear to be feasible alternatives, but they merely serve as substitutes, exchanging one form of nicotine consumption for another. While they might provide temporary respite for physical cravings, they fail to address the fundamental psychological components of addiction. The objective of this approach is not to replace one form of addiction with another, but rather to liberate oneself from the perpetual cycle of dependence altogether.

Schemes and expedient remedies offer the allure of effortless and immediate outcomes, yet frequently fall short in attaining sustained achievements. This approach promotes a heightened level of introspection and deliberation, equipping you with the necessary resources to navigate the intricacies of addiction and establish a steadfast groundwork for enduring transformation.

What Is The Financial Revenue Generated By The Tobacco Industry?

The tobacco sector represents a prominent and highly lucrative segment among global industries. Based on multiple assessments, the tobacco industry at a global scale holds considerable monetary value, amounting to billions of dollars, and is accountable for the production and distribution of billions of cigarettes annually.

The tobacco industry in the United States alone generates an annual revenue exceeding $100 billion. This can predominantly be attributed to the substantial demand for tobacco products, notwithstanding the manifold health hazards associated with smoking. The sector comprises prominent tobacco corporations like Philip Morris International, British American Tobacco, and Japan Tobacco International, alongside a multitude of smaller enterprises and distributors.

The tobacco industry possesses a lengthy and captivating chronicle, commencing in the 16th century with the initial introduction of tobacco to Europe. Throughout the years, the industry has undergone significant advancements and expansion, resulting in increased intricacy and structure within its marketing and distribution methodologies. Currently, the tobacco industry holds significant influence in the global economy, with its financial gains steadily increasing despite the prevalence of various health advisories and escalating regulatory measures.

The tobacco industry has achieved considerable success due to its adeptness in effectively promoting its products to a diverse spectrum of consumers. The sector employs a range of strategies, encompassing advertising and sponsorship, to specifically cater to distinct demographics, notably youth and female segments. Furthermore, the industry has effectively engaged in advocacy efforts to counteract the implementation of anti-smoking legislation and regulations, oftentimes managing to impede or dilute the impact of such measures.

Notwithstanding its accomplishments, the tobacco sector encounters a multitude of obstacles and critiques. Numerous health organizations and governmental bodies across the globe are actively engaged in efforts aimed at diminishing the demand for tobacco products and enhancing public knowledge regarding the detrimental health consequences associated with smoking. Moreover, an increasing number of nations have implemented tax measures and regulatory policies targeting tobacco products, aiming to mitigate the prevalence of smoking and alleviate the consequential burden on public health expenditures.

To summarize, the tobacco industry maintains a significant presence in the worldwide economy, yielding billions of dollars in annual profits. Notwithstanding the increasingly stringent regulations and the dissemination of health warnings, the industry persists in expanding its operations and promoting its products to a diverse clientele. The sustainability of the industry in the coming years is yet to be determined, as global governments and health organizations are actively striving to curtail the consumption of tobacco products and advocate for a more health-conscious way of living.

9: The Role of Nutrition in Promoting Health and Well-being

T

The Influence of Dietary Habits on Smoking Cessation: Nourishments that Diminish Cravings and Facilitate Detoxification of the Body.

1: The Influence of Dietary Factors on the Cessation of Smoking

1.1 Exploring the Correlation between Diet and Smoking Cessation

The dietary choices we make can have a profound influence on our general health and well-being, encompassing our capacity to quit smoking effectively. A nutritious diet can contribute to the reduction of cravings, facilitate the body's detoxification, uplift mood, and foster overall robustness. Directing one's attention towards nutrition and conscientiously selecting food can enhance the likelihood of attaining a smoke-free existence.

1.2 Supporting Detoxification

The act of smoking introduces a multitude of toxins and noxious chemicals into the human body. The incorporation of nutrient-dense foods into one's diet can facilitate the elimination of these harmful toxins while bolstering the body's inherent detoxification mechanisms. Through the inclusion of certain food items in your dietary intake, it is possible to augment the functionality of your liver, facilitate optimal digestion, and assist in the elimination of toxins acquired from the habit of smoking.

2: Nutritional Options to Alleviate Cravings and Facilitate the Process of Smoking Cessation

Section 2.1: Fresh Produce

Fresh fruits and vegetables offer a plethora of nutrients and are rich in vital vitamins, minerals, and antioxidants that contribute to the enhancement of general health and wellness. Additionally, they provide a delightful crispness and inherent sweetness that can effectively mitigate desires for confectioneries or nutritionally deficient snacks. Integrate an assortment of vibrant fruits and vegetables into your meals and snacks to ensure that your body receives the essential nourishment it requires.

2.2 Whole Grains

Whole grains, including quinoa, brown rice, oats, and whole wheat bread, are highly beneficial sources of complex carbohydrates and dietary fiber. They offer long-lasting sustenance, promote glucose regulation, and contribute to a prolonged feeling of satiety. The incorporation of whole grains into your dietary regimen can contribute to a decrease in cravings and mitigate the occurrence of energy crashes, which can potentially engender the inclination to smoke.

2.3 Lean Proteins

Lean sources of protein, including poultry such as chicken and turkey, fish, legumes like beans and lentils, and soy-based products like tofu, are fundamental components in the process of smoking cessation. They offer indispensable amino acids that facilitate the process of muscle regeneration and upkeep, enhance metabolic activity, and help you maintain a feeling of satisfaction. Incorporating lean proteins into your meals has the potential to stabilize your blood sugar levels, foster a sensation of satiety, and decrease the probability of cravings occurring.

2.4 Omega-3 Fatty Acids

Omega-3 fatty acids, which occur naturally in oily fish such as salmon, mackerel, and sardines, as well as in walnuts, flaxseeds, and chia seeds, possess anti-inflammatory attributes and bolster cognitive function. They have the potential to effectively mitigate cravings and enhance overall mood, thus offering noteworthy advantages during the cessation process. Incorporate these beneficial fatty ingredients into your dietary routine to enhance your holistic health.

2.5 The Influence of Herbal Teas on Hydration

Herbal infusions like green tea, chamomile, or ginger tea, can serve as a calming and hydrating substitute for smoking. They provide an assortment of flavors and potential advantages, encompassing stress reduction, enhancement of digestive processes, and facilitation of relaxation. Ensuring proper hydration by consuming water, herbal teas, and infused water on a regular basis can effectively mitigate cravings and promote overall well-being.

Conclusion:

The importance of nutrition and maintaining a healthy diet cannot be overstated when it comes to achieving success in smoking cessation. By consciously selecting nutritious food options and integrating specific foods into your dietary regimen, you can facilitate the cessation process, diminish longing for substances, and elevate your overall state of wellness. Fresh produce, whole grains, low-fat proteins, essential omega-3 fatty acids, and herbal infusions are amongst the dietary options known to alleviate cravings and facilitate the detoxification process within the body. Please ensure to maintain proper hydration and attentively heed your body's cues of thirst and satiety. In the forthcoming and concluding chapter, we shall synthesize all the components expounded upon in this electronic book and offer pragmatic suggestions, methodologies, and a comprehensive approach to assist you in your endeavor to attain a smoke-free lifestyle.

Enhancing your commitment to being smoke-free.

While proceeding with your pursuit of a smoke-free existence, it is vital to reassess and reshape your self-perception as an individual who abstains from smoking. Adopting this new identity can serve to reinforce your dedication to maintaining a smoke-free lifestyle and facilitate the resistance of cravings and prevention of relapse. Allow me to provide you with a few suggestions on how to enhance your smokeless lifestyle:

A. Engage in the cultivation of fresh interests and pastimes: The active pursuit of novel activities can aid in the establishment of a distinct and independent identity, detached from the habit of smoking. Partake in pursuits that are incongruous with smoking, such as engaging in physical fitness, culinary activities, or attending smoke-free gatherings.

B. Establish new connections: Cultivating fresh social bonds or enhancing preexisting relationships with individuals who do not smoke can serve to reaffirm your non-smoking identity. Engage in the exploration of social gatherings or communities that align with your passions and principles.

C. Undertake a thorough reassessment of your values and priorities: Contemplate the facets of your life that hold utmost significance to you and deliberate on the harmonization between your smoke-free way of living and these values. This could potentially entail reassessing your professional endeavors, interpersonal connections, or individual aspirations in order to align them with your commitment to maintaining a smoke-free lifestyle.

D. Disseminate information regarding the advantages of smoking cessation: Disseminate your personal insights and expertise to individuals who are contemplating quitting smoking or encountering difficulties in maintaining a smoke-free lifestyle. By providing assistance to others, you strengthen your dedication to maintaining a smoke-free lifestyle and contribute to a wider ethos of vitality and wellness.

Engaging in continuous learning and pursuing personal development

Remaining abstinent from smoking is not a singular occurrence, but rather a lifelong journey of acquiring knowledge and personal development. As you progress further on your expedition, it is imperative to remain receptive to novel concepts, encounters, and methodologies that facilitate the preservation of your tobacco-free condition. Presented below are several suggestions for fostering a commitment to continuous learning and personal development:

A. Maintain up-to-date knowledge regarding the most recent studies and advancements associated with smoking cessation and tobacco control. This can assist individuals in remaining informed about novel approaches, therapies, and support systems aimed at maintaining a smoke-free lifestyle.

B. Embrace the concept of being receptive to change and demonstrating adaptability. Acknowledge the potential for shifts in your needs, preferences, and circumstances as time progresses, and demonstrate a readiness to adapt your strategies for maintaining a smoke-free lifestyle accordingly.

C. Consistently evaluate your objectives and advancement. Conduct regular assessments of your progress in maintaining a smoke-free lifestyle to pinpoint areas of achievement and areas that can be enhanced. Utilize this data to enhance your strategies and uphold your steadfast dedication to sustaining a smoke-free lifestyle.

D. Engage in the pursuit of novel challenges and diverse experiences. Participate in endeavors that challenge you beyond your familiar boundaries and foster individual development. This can aid in the cultivation of your self-assurance, fortitude, and ability to effectively navigate the obstacles encountered while maintaining a smoke-free lifestyle.

In conclusion, maintaining a smoke-free lifestyle is a lifelong endeavor that necessitates unwavering commitment, flexibility, and perpetual personal development. By adopting the methods and principles elucidated in this chapter, you can effectively uphold your smoke-free condition and reap the manifold advantages of a healthier and more gratifying existence. Please bear in mind that your dedication to maintaining a smoke-free lifestyle not only serves as a personal investment in your own physical and mental wellness, but also offers motivation and encouragement to individuals who may be contemplating embarking on this transformative journey.

Benefits derived from the cessation of tobacco use

We are striving to present a comprehensive overview of the immediate advantages associated with smoking cessation, as evidenced by extensive research conducted on individuals who have successfully quit.

● Subsequent to a 20-minute intermission for smoking, the heart rate commences a decline. After a period of twelve hours following cessation,

● The carbon monoxide levels revert to their usual state. After a duration of approximately two to three weeks, there is a notable enhancement in both blood circulation and lung function.

● The act of smoking primarily leads to respiratory conditions, such as persistent coughing, which is exacerbated by smoking. Smoking contributes to the exacerbation of bronchitis symptoms.

● The act of smoking has a pronounced adverse effect on individuals suffering from asthma. Even individuals in good health have been observed to exhibit diminished breathing.

because of ongoing smoking. It has been observed that specific physiological concerns persist for a period of one to nine months following the cessation of smoking. Nevertheless, a discernible enhancement may become evident.

Some immediate Yield

The mortality rates associated with lung and oral cancer in the United States have shown a continuous decline, indicative of a diminishing pattern. This occurrence has incited numerous States to embrace comparable policies and execute them with heightened enthusiasm and vigor. Thirteen states have enacted legislation prohibiting smoking in public places and workplaces. It is worth noting, however, that only a limited number of these states have implemented similar restrictions in bars, thereby indicating a gradual advancement in this area. Nevertheless, it is important to acknowledge that numerous objectives are yet to be achieved.

A limited number of individuals confine this practice solely to establishments of an exclusive nature, such as restaurants or bars. While regulations prohibiting the sale of tobacco to minors are in effect across all 50 states and the District of Columbia, their implementation has been negligible in practice.

Approximately 70% of actively smoking individuals choose to quit, a majority of whom, at minimum, 45%, decide to do so as a result of personal reasons before succumbing to the deadly entrapment of smoking once again. A mere 2.5% of smokers have the potential to achieve the pinnacle of success each year by successfully and permanently quitting smoking. Quitting smoking offers substantial and prompt health benefits for individuals of all genders and age groups. When individuals cease smoking prior to reaching 50 years of age, their likelihood of mortality being lowered by approximately half during the ensuing 15-year period.

When compared to individuals who continue to engage in smoking.

AHCPR implemented measures.

The findings of the expert panel affiliated with the Awareness via Mass Communication and Rectification (AHCPR), an agency under the purview of the Agency for Healthcare Research and Quality, establish that diverse measures have proven effective in eliciting motivation among individuals.

● A therapist's straightforward counsel induces 30% of individuals to actively contemplate cessation of this detrimental behavior.

● The involvement in counseling, be it on an individual or group basis, significantly increases the likelihood of successful cessation.

● Approximately 40% of individuals have been reached via telephonic helplines and support services.

● The residual aspects are addressed through the implementation of nicotine replacement therapy. In order to address addiction and attain complete autonomy from smoking, supplementary services such as pharmacotherapy and psychotherapy are provided at an additional cost.

● Occupations in the fields of manual labor, food service, and various other service-related industries

Detection and capture by the National Cancer Institute

● The presence of harmful secondhand smoke in work environments was found to endanger 46 percent of individuals employed in blue-collar, food service, and other service industry occupations.

● Adolescents, constituting 22% of the total workforce of 5.5 million individuals, face a significantly elevated risk, 50% greater, compared to the general populace, of succumbing to lung cancer.

● Implementation of appropriate policies, strategic planning, efficient process execution, and adoption of evidence-based clinical and educational methodologies have the potential to significantly reduce the general public's inadvertent exposure to secondhand smoke. Strategies regarding public policy encompassing robust clean indoor air regulations, stringent workplace restrictions, and the effective implementation of limitations for safeguarding public health.

● Extensive endeavors through public awareness campaigns and localized community initiatives have yielded significant reductions in the exposure of both adults and children to the harmful effects of secondhand smoke in public environments.

By eliminating passive voice, an outcome that can be expected is a reduction in respiratory illnesses and related conditions among children, leading to a significant decrease in the number of doctor visits, which amount to approximately 500,000 annually, due to worsening asthma.

Consequently, the American Academy of Pediatrics has recommended that healthcare professionals increase parental awareness regarding the hazards of secondhand smoke on the developing respiratory system, and provide guidance on safeguarding children from this perilous healthcare issue.

Beginning To Comprehend The Addictive Substance

Nicotine, an inherent chemical constituent commonly present in the leaves of tobacco plants, serves as the principal addictive factor contributing to the addictive properties of cigarettes and related tobacco commodities. It is categorized as a stimulant substance owing to its impact on the central nervous system, with a particular focus on the brain. Gaining insight into the scientific principles governing nicotine and its physiological effects can provide illumination as to the reasons underlying its significant potency and addictive nature.

Chemical Properties of Nicotine:

Nicotine is classified as an alkaloid, which falls within the category of organic compounds. The substance is an odoriferous liquid of an oily nature, devoid of any color. Nicotine, in its undiluted state, possesses significant toxicity; however, when present in minute quantities within tobacco products, it functions as a powerful psychoactive compound.

Absorption and Distribution:

Upon inhalation of tobacco smoke, nicotine rapidly penetrates the bloodstream via the pulmonary route. The significantly perfused lung tissue enables swift uptake, thereby enabling nicotine to rapidly traverse to the brain in a matter of seconds. In addition, nicotine can be assimilated via the mucous membranes of the oral cavity, nasal passages, or dermis when utilizing smokeless tobacco items or nicotine substitution therapies. After entering the bloodstream, nicotine permeates the entire body, exerting its influence on multiple organs and systems. By virtue of its lipophilic properties, the compound readily penetrates the blood-brain barrier, facilitating direct modulation of cerebral activities.

Mechanism of Action:

Nicotine achieves its impacts through its interaction with distinct receptors in the brain referred to as nicotinic acetylcholine receptors (nAChRs). These receptors are extensively dispersed throughout the brain and perform a crucial function in a multitude of physiological processes, encompassing cognition, mood modulation, and the pathways involved in reward.

When nicotine actively interacts with nicotinic acetylcholine receptors (nAChRs), it initiates the subsequent release of various neurotransmitters, particularly dopamine. Dopamine is correlated with sensations of gratification, incentive, and drive. The enhanced dopamine release elicited by nicotine plays a pivotal role in the amplification of rewarding outcomes and the subsequent formation of addictive behaviors.

Reward Pathway and Reinforcement:

The addictive nature of nicotine stems from its capacity to induce dopamine release in the brain's reward circuitry. The reward pathway, predominantly centeredaround the ventral tegmental area (VTA) and the nucleus accumbens (NAc), constitutes a intricate circuitry of brain regions that govern the perception of pleasure and the facilitation of behaviors through positive reinforcement. When nicotine stimulates the reward circuitry, it induces a gratifying sensation commonly known as a 'nicotine rush'. This sensation serves to strengthen the habit of smoking, thus increasing the likelihood of individuals persisting in smoking to experience the reinforcing effects.

Development of Tolerance:

With continued and frequent exposure to nicotine, the brain undergoes adaptations characterized by the decrement in the quantity of accessible nicotinic acetylcholine receptors (nAChRs) and the desensitization of the remaining receptor population. This process culminates in the establishment of tolerance, which necessitates higher doses of nicotine to attain comparable effects. The desensitization of nicotinic acetylcholine receptors (nAChRs) additionally plays a role in fostering nicotine addiction. When the concentration of nicotine declines, individuals encounter the manifestation of cravings and withdrawal symptoms, as the cerebral faculties necessitate a greater amount of nicotine to sustain a state of equilibrium.

Withdrawal and Cravings:

The hallmark of nicotine addiction is the manifestation of withdrawal symptoms upon the discontinuation or decrease in nicotine consumption. The aforementioned symptoms may encompass irritability, anxiety, restlessness, impaired concentration, heightened appetite, and strong cravings for nicotine.

Withdrawal symptoms manifest as a result of the brain's adaptation to the lack of nicotine and the disruption of the intricate equilibrium in neurotransmitter function. Desires, specifically, possess a compelling and formidable nature, posing resistance as a challenge, due to the brain's association of nicotine with gratification and incentives.

MANAGING CIGARETTE DESIRES IMMEDIATELY

Locate an oral alternative – Ensure that you have a variety of items readily available to be consumed whenever cravings arise. Consider trying breath mints, carrot or celery sticks, chewing gum, or sunflower seeds. Alternatively, one could opt to consume a beverage using a drinking straw.

Engage your mind in activities – Browse through a book or magazine, immerse yourself in your favorite music, solve a crossword or Sudoku puzzle, or indulge in an online game.

Engage in manual activities to occupy your hands - Utilizing stress balls, pencils, or origami can serve as suitable alternatives to satisfy the need for tactile sensations.

Maintain oral hygiene by brushing your teeth - Regularly brushing your teeth with proper technique can aid in eliminating cigarette cravings.

Consume water gradually by drinking a substantial glass. Not only will it aid in curbing one's hunger, but maintaining proper hydration also helps to alleviate the symptoms of nicotine withdrawal.

Ignite an alternate item – Instead of igniting a cigarette, ignite a flame or a fragrant incense stick.

Engage in physical activity – Embark on a leisurely stroll, perform jumping jacks or pushups, engage in yoga stretches, or take a brisk walk around the neighborhood.

Make an effort to unwind - Engage in activities that promote a sense of calmness, such as engaging in personal hygiene routines, engaging in reflective thinking, reading a book, or practicing mindfulness through deep breathing exercises.

Refrain from engaging in smoking activities in areas where it is prohibited – Seek refuge in a public edifice, establishment, commercial complex, coffeehouse, or theater, for instance.

Types of Smoke

Smoking is a widespread phenomenon on a global scale, with empirical evidence indicating that approximately 1.3 billion individuals engage in daily smoking habits. Nevertheless, regardless of the method by which one consumes smoke - whether through chewing, sniffing, inhaling, or smoking - there is no distinction or imposition of restrictions on the associated risks.

Smoking represents a manifestation of addiction, illness, infirmity, and other facets that are financially, physically, and energetically extravagant.

Cannabis smoking devices, whether they be of traditional or electronic nature, come with a considerable price tag ranging from approximately $10 to

$300. Suppose you consume approximately 3 grams of smokeable substance on a daily basis, equating to an expenditure of approximately $30. Consider the extent to which your income is allocated towards purchasing tobacco products. What is it? 50%?Or more?

Let us examine the different kinds of smoke at our disposal.

- Cigar and pipes

- Cigarette

- Hand-rolled tobacco products known as bidis and clove cigars

- Hookah, and Shisha

- Cigar with a mild and refreshing menthol flavor

- Chewy Tobacco

- Electronic cigarette

Disregard the assertion that "what is damaged can't be repaired." I assure you that regardless of the duration you have engaged in smoking, chewing tobacco, or inhaling substances, it is possible for you to permanently quit.

Given your newfound awareness of the minimal distinctions between these smoke types, let us now delve into the potential motives that drive your participation in this ambivalent pursuit.

What is the underlying reason for your decision to engage in smoking?

As individuals, we possess an inherent desire for heightened gratification and contentment, thereby occasionally succumbing to the allure of superficial allure.

We often disregard the genuine essence of happiness and fulfillment, instead opting for a preoccupation with various forms of addiction, such as overindulgence in food and lifestyle choices, excessive reliance on smartphones, and in your specific circumstance, the habit of smoking.

Indeed, when one derives pleasure from their activities, a signal is transmitted to the brain, kindling a desire for further experiences imbued with such gratification.

Hence, our affinity for cookies, intimacy, cuisine, attire, tobacco, and liquor occurs infrequently. Subsequently, an addiction ensues, necessitating diligent and steadfast efforts to conquer.

The persistent yearnings persist, akin to an influx of intense excitement, eliciting an altered and subconscious aspect of your being that previously remained unacknowledged, all in the pursuit of fulfilling those desires.

The sensation of desiring additional stimuli arises from the presence of DOPAMINE, a neurochemical secreted by the brain that elicits pleasurable sensations. An excess of dopamine results in the condition of addiction.

Dopamine plays a crucial role in ensuring individual survival. It governs a broad range of bodily functions, encompassing cognition and focus, motor control, emotional well-being, circadian rhythms, cardiovascular health, renal activity, lactation, cardiac rhythm, pain modulation, and notably, cognitive focus.

Allow me to elucidate: When one possesses an optimal level of dopamine, it is undoubtedly beneficial for both the body and the brain. However, dopamine recognizes and seeks out pleasurable experiences, persistently desiring to replicate that sensation. Nevertheless, in the event that you resist the temptation, the release of dopamine within your system redirects towards alternative regions of your physiology, providing gratification elsewhere.

Dopamine transmits signals between different anatomical regions, subsequently relaying information to the brain. It instills a sense of gratification, drive, and contentment stemming from one's actions, perceptions, and sources of enjoyment.

Having a diminished level of dopamine is not conducive to an optimal state. It induces a decreased sense of motivation, hesitancy, fatigue, restlessness, and low mood, ultimately diminishing the capacity to experience joy.

Additionally, it is possible to experience an excessive elevation of dopamine levels in a specific region of the body relative to others. This imbalance may result in the emergence of addictive behaviors, aggression, compulsive overeating, impulsive spending, and an exaggerated sense of competitiveness.

Cigarette smoking leads to an elevation in dopamine levels as a consequence of the substantial nicotine content, thereby cultivating a desire for additional nicotine intake. You may inquire, "What is nicotine?"

Nicotine is the primary factor contributing to the challenge of smoking cessation. It is a highly habit-forming compound present in cigarettes, tobacco, and vaping commodities. It exhibits addictive properties due to its ability to trigger neuronal signaling upon entering the circulatory system, resulting in the subsequent release of dopamine within the brain. Keep in mind that the brain retains what it is nourished with. Let us discuss a few potential factors that may have prompted you to initiate smoking:

Peer Pressure

Another potential contributing factor to your smoking habit could be the influence and pressure exerted by your peers. The narrative has had a profound impact on individuals, serving as an explanation for their inclination towards various pursuits, particularly indulgent behaviors. The social influence exerted by acquaintances of various age groups, whether similar or disparate, manifests as a discreet yet compelling force that compels individuals to seek a sense of belonging.

Please bear in mind that it is perfectly acceptable to not conform to societal norms, and it is truly commendable when one finds contentment in embracing their authentic self.

Stress reduction; anger and discomfort regulation; tranquility

It is a well-established fact that smoking provides a temporary respite from stress, negative emotions, and fosters a sense of tranquility. The fast-paced nature of modern society can compel individuals to search for solace by resorting to the gratification provided by tobacco consumption. It is also conceivable that one engages in smoking as a means of combating stage fright, anxiety, and timidity.

Temporal Distortion Effect - The cessation of nicotine induces significant distortion in the perception of time. Once you resolve to cease this habit, you will experience cravings which, albeit ephemeral, may seemingly endure indefinitely within your psyche. Ensure that you possess a wrist timepiece that is practical for accurately maintaining a sincere perception of time. It is important to recognize that it is possible to observe multiple usage cues simultaneously. However, these skills are quite uncommon and this fact should be regarded as a positive development rather than a negative one. Episode Frequency Desired - It is expected that the individuals undergoing the most challenging stage of their recovery will ideally witness at least six episodes within the third day. This equates to a total of 18 minutes of strenuous labor on your most demanding day. What will happen if you are unable to meet the requirement referred to as "minimum"?

Are you capable of enduring approximately 35 minutes of a demanding situation, wherein the conscious mind is filled with evident anxiety, aiming to regain control over your mental state, physical well-being, and overall life circumstances? Absolutely! We all can. Make the necessary preparations for the forthcoming days of being free from nicotine. Furthermore, it is essential to remain vigilant for subtle variations in stimuli that prompt intense desires. Comprehending the Significant Aspiration - The individual who quits at the lowest frequency witnesses approximately 1.5 instances of desired outcomes per day over a span of 11 days. It can feel akin to being subjected to an unexpected and forceful blow.

Embrace Desires - Another effective coping strategy involves intellectually expanding and fully embracing the longing. It is customary for one to experience impulses, however, it is imperative not to perceive them as catastrophic events; instead, one should strive to endure and exhibit discipline. In the sphere of one's intellectual pursuits, encapsulate and embrace the amalgamation of longing, unease, and resilience, only to witness their gradual dissipation and ultimate demise within one's very grasp.

Behave appropriately, extend greetings, and conquer your fears. Rather than fleeing from your fears, it is crucial for you to confront and conquer them. The sole relinquishment required from you is the relinquishment of nicotine. Additionally, it is important to refrain from consuming alcohol. It is pertinent to mention that alcohol usage is known to be linked with 50% of all diseases, although you may already be aware of this information. Exercise extreme caution regarding the consumption of alcoholic beverages during the initial week. Incorporating a substance that weakens self-control, and subsequently engaging with individuals who are accustomed to nicotine, all while still grappling with the early stages of withdrawal, is a strategy that is conducive to failure. Establish a solid foundation for repossession from the outset. If you possess knowledge and experience regarding the consumption of alcohol, when you are prepared to address and execute your cues for drinking or smoking, it is advisable to consciously divide the challenge into more specific categories of triggers. Make an effort to consume beverages in a nicotine-free environment within the confines of your own home. You are encouraged to socialize with friends, but it is advised to abstain from both drinking and smoking during these outings. Alternatively, it is recommended to moderate your alcohol intake by interspersing it with intervals of consuming water or other non-alcoholic beverages. In order to effectively accomplish your objective, it is imperative to establish a comprehensive strategy. Without a strategic framework and a defined objective, you are bound to meet with inevitable failure. Structured strategizing is not discretionary; rather, it is imperative to achieve the objective of cessation of the smoking habit. It is advisable that individuals attempting to abstain from alcohol consider simultaneously abstaining from both alcohol and nicotine, as this approach is likely to yield more favorable outcomes. There is no legitimate justification for reverting back to previous behavior - It is important to acknowledge that nicotine consumption cannot serve as a remedy to any difficult situation. We must acknowledge the reality that no legitimate justification exists for any type of regression, be it engaging with others, experiencing a difficult day, losing interest in activities, facing stress, taking leisure time, consuming alcohol, being involved in a car accident, encountering financial difficulties, going through a breakup, quitting a job, being subjected to armed robbery, enduring a hurricane or earthquake, surviving a severe storm or flood, welcoming a new addition to the family, or eventually losing our loved ones.

There is an absence of taste buds in the human lungs. There was no discernible distinction between nicotine addiction rehabilitation and alcoholism recovery. Resist the enticements of succumbing to the allure of "Just One Last Time." Succumbing to this temptation will exacerbate the challenges associated with overcoming your addiction. It is worth noting that with just a single inhalation, the illusion of having never quit smoking will be effortlessly created. This phenomenon occurs as a result of the neurological gateways, which are linked to smoking, being reopened by the act of taking a single puff. Nicotine inundates the brain with dopamine, exacerbating the challenge of overcoming the addiction beyond the initial attempt. It is imperative that you refrain from reverting back to your previous sense of self. Your previous persona was an individual who was unable to cease the act of smoking. Your newfound identity involves an individual who comprehends that tobacco usage will not impede your life's purpose. Reward Yourself with Meaningful Achievements - Instead of spending money on cigarettes, set aside those funds and invest in personal growth to attain something truly desired within a week, a month, or even a year. Engage in pursuits that align with your interests and keep you occupied, thus maintaining distance from your addictive tendencies. Engaging in additional activities that enhance productivity can significantly reduce the amount of time dedicated to contemplating smoking. Please contemplate the potential of having radiant teeth and feeling uninhibited when expressing laughter or smiling in public, or arrange for a thoracic radiography to address any concerns regarding the potential consequences of prolonged delay. Refrain from relying on any form of crutches - A crutch refers to any reliance on compensation that is contingent upon completion, and if abruptly withdrawn, could potentially lead to a loss of support and regression. It is crucial to ensure that you do not associate yourself with an individual who has recently resigned while you are still in the process of recuperation. This approach poses a significant risk and is highly likely to undermine all the progress you have made in your recovery. While it is beneficial to have supportive individuals in close proximity, it is advisable to select someone who has been smoke-free for an extensive period or a non-smoker to rely on for support. Your tobacco dependency holds significant value for the nicotine addiction industry, as it results in substantial financial losses totaling in the thousands. The media seeks to dissuade individuals from abstaining from their addiction. The incessant promotion of nicotine advertisements with the intention of enticing individuals to purchase the multitude of tobacco products, which are well-acknowledged to lack any health benefits and instead pose a detriment to our physical well-being. Contained within the captivating assortment of vividly hued containers, tin cans, and enclosures, and secured by more than 600 distinct flavor enhancements, resides the chemical compound widely regarded by addiction specialists as the planet's most alluring. Irrespective of the duration of tobacco use, individuals need not experience the sensation of being confined within their own corporeal vessel. They are no longer obligated to assume the role of a disadvantaged party due to the presence of the cigarette. There exist methods to conquer this addiction and unleash the utmost manifestation of your being that has remained latent throughout these years. The cigarette is undeniably repulsive and exceptionally lethal, particularly due to the adverse effects of nicotine. Nicotine not only infiltrates one of the most potent carcinogens known as NNK, but it also possesses considerable toxicity, gradually proving to be more lethal than the venom of diamondback python snakes or cyanide. Please take this information about nicotine into account. A mere dosage of approximately 40-59 mg of pure nicotine, equivalent to a small quantity ranging from 2-3 drops, exhibits the potential lethality to an individual of typical constitution. On each occasion an individual smokes a cigarette, they introduce 1 mg of nicotine into their physiological system. They have a strong affinity for such behavior due to its necessity in maintaining proper nourishment of a progressively declining level of nicotine within their bloodstream, which typically decreases at a consistent rate of every two hours. Once an individual develops a dependence on Nicotine, an increasing dosage is required to achieve the desired physiological response within the bloodstream. As the frequency of utilization increases, so does our reliance on it to yield the desired outcome. In this scenario, individuals experience the detrimental effects of nicotine as it enters their bloodstream, establishing a subsequent dependency that necessitates another intake in due time. Let us observe a situation in which acid is generated, such as the rapid neutralization of the body's nicotine restriction due to stress and alcohol consumption. As one observes their surroundings in everyday life, one will undoubtedly come across individuals who exhibit a persistent inclination towards the habitual act of smoking. For instance, in the current instant, you are engaging in the act of perusing and carefully contemplating the subject matter, but most likely not experiencing a desire or craving for nicotine. Contemplation of retrieval is beneficial rather than detrimental, as it serves to circumvent any potential grievances.

Non-Smoker or Ex-Smoker? May I kindly request that you provide identification for the purpose of verifying your identity? Nobody in

Now, may I inquire about the specific date you have selected as your ultimate cessation date?

Conquer Withdrawal Symptoms And Cravings

To successfully cease smoking, it is imperative that one possess a resolute determination. Quitting is always a challenging task. Indeed, a significant number of individuals who smoke have made attempts on no less than a hundred occasions. They also encountered failure on a hundred occasions. The true difficulty lies in devising strategies to overcome the withdrawal symptoms and cravings in a holistic manner.

You may be curious as to the implications of smoking. What factors contribute to the challenge of quitting smoking? It proved to be a formidable task due to the primary constituent of the cigarette. The aforementioned substance is nicotine, which significantly exacerbates the challenges associated with quitting. Additionally, it enhances the overall enjoyment of smoking. Abstaining from smoking causes the nicotine present in your bloodstream to transmit signals to your brain, initiating an inclination or yearning for it.

Nicotine cessation results in a variety of symptoms. It typically commences within a few hours after cessation. The culmination should be anticipated within a time frame of forty-eight to seventy-two hours following the cessation of cigarette consumption. There are instances when the symptoms become evident for a few consecutive days. For individuals who are not directly affected, the duration of the experience may extend for a period spanning several weeks. It is contingent upon the extent to which you were engaged in the act of smoking.

In the event that you are experiencing withdrawal syndrome, it is important to bear in mind that it is a natural occurrence to encounter unpleasant and uncomfortable sensations. There are instances when one experiences a sense of incongruity with their true self. It constitutes an integral component of the expedition. It is imperative to bear in mind that this too shall come to pass. After approximately one month, you will find it amusing and easily dismiss it. You have the ability to move forward and put the negative experience in the past. Nevertheless, it is imperative that during the period in which you continue to experience the consequences of cessation, you must comprehend the subsequent aspects:

It is entirely customary to experience the urge. It serves as a mechanism through which your body expresses its intention to replenish the nicotine levels in your bloodstream. The desire typically endures for a brief duration of a few minutes. After approximately one week, you will experience a reduction in these symptoms. Maintain a strong sense of resolute determination. Allow me to offer a practical suggestion: In the event of experiencing a craving, it may prove beneficial to openly acknowledge it. It will serve as a helpful reminder of your commitment to permanently cease smoking. Communicate the information to a close acquaintance or a relative. If you happen to find yourself in a solitary state amid the circumstances, endeavor to engage in a numerical recitation ranging from one to one hundred, or until such time that the inclination subsides. Please be advised that it will take a few minutes for it to subside.

*) You may encounter some difficulty in attaining your typical degree of focus. However, there is no need for concern regarding this matter. In due course, you will acquire the capacity to focus. Nicotine is widely thought to facilitate the enhancement of attention for numerous individuals. The act of cessation could be interpreted as a diminishment in the ability to focus. However, it is not precisely the situation. The cognitive haziness you are experiencing is a direct result of the lack of nicotine. In due course, the condition is poised to ameliorate as your brain will experience an augmented level of oxygenation owing to an enhanced circulatory system. However, when faced with circumstances that make it particularly difficult to maintain focus,

one can mitigate the issue by creating a comprehensive list or effectively organizing their activities. In certain instances, individuals who have quit smoking may encounter challenges in achieving restful sleep. For individuals who experience it, fatigue can arise as a consequence of insufficient sleep. This represents a frequently encountered occurrence of withdrawal symptoms. As nicotine has the capacity to elevate metabolic functioning, the cessation of smoking abruptly terminates the momentum of the metabolic processes. As a result of this, the modified metabolic rate gives rise to disrupted sleep patterns. Please take note that, similar to the preceding points discussed in this section of the chapter, this phenomenon will eventually come to an end.

It is acceptable to experience occasional episodes of irritability. If you engage in the act of smoking, it is advisable to inform individuals in your vicinity about your circumstances. Why? If the situation arises where you may lose control in the future, they should be provided with adequate contextualization and clarification. Inform them about the circumstances you are currently experiencing. Given one's adherence to honesty, it is uncertain what the outcome may be. They may even exhibit support for the idea.

Withdrawing from activities significantly diminishes your quality of life.

The propensity for smoking can be exceedingly robust, and attempting to cease this habit can present a highly formidable endeavor. It constitutes an additional challenge as smoking tends to become ingrained in one's mundane routines, effortlessly intertwined with the most habitual activities one engages in. If such is the current situation, then it is imperative for you to apply additional endeavor. By implementing these strategies, you can mitigate the impact of nicotine withdrawal:" "By employing these methods, you can employ measures to mitigate the consequences of nicotine withdrawal:" "By adopting these approaches, you can effectively minimize the repercussions of nicotine withdrawal:

*) Endeavor to implement a significant alteration to your daily routines. If you are accustomed to smoking following your meals, it may be advantageous to refrain from lingering in the dining area. Please return to your designated workspace promptly. Adopt an

alternative practice - engage in conversation with your colleagues instead. If you find yourself with additional free time, consider taking a leisurely stroll instead of engaging in the act of smoking.

*) Refrain from exposing yourself to circumstances in which you anticipate experiencing the desire. This holds great significance, particularly in the initial phase of withdrawal.

*) Frequenting establishments with a strict no-smoking policy. By immersing oneself in the cultural and educational environment offered by museums, libraries, churches, and theaters, one can effectively divert their attention away from smoking.

*) Please designate your vehicle and residence as areas where smoking is

prohibited. By taking this approach, you will find increased motivation to chart a divergent course.

Please be aware that smoking is an exceedingly costly practice. Not solely due to the necessity of monetary resources for purchasing cigarettes, but also on account of the health implications associated with their consumption. Therefore, whenever you experience a sense of triumph in your decision to quit and you achieve significant milestones in your journey (such as completing the first week without smoking, reaching six months, or accomplishing a full year), it is essential to appropriately compensate yourself. Take pride in yourself and find joy in your accomplishments. And display magnanimity in overcoming an unsightly vice.

The Adverse Consequences Of Smoking And The Rationale For Smoking Cessation

Effects of Smoking Cigarettes

Diminishment of gustatory and olfactory sensations.

The act of smoking tobacco cigarettes leads to a reduction in the smoker's olfactory and gustatory perception. Physicians commonly attribute the desensitization of sensory perceptions to the act of smoking. This phenomenon is actually substantiated by the fact that when smokers cease their habit, they often report an improvement in their olfactory and gustatory perception. Individuals who engage in smoking may encounter difficulties in perceiving and discerning the flavors of food, as well as detecting various scents, regardless of their desirability. The reduced olfactory perception is, in fact, held responsible for the concomitant decrease in gustatory perception. The gradual decline of these senses implies that cigarette smokers will not perceive it as strongly and will instead adapt to the diminished sensation.

Faster Ageing

The act of smoking cigarettes is correlated with the early onset of aging in individuals who engage in this habit. The presence of facial wrinkles, gaunt cheeks, and discolored hands and lips are among the common manifestations observed in individuals who engage in tobacco smoking. The act of smoking cigarettes is associated with the narrowing of blood vessels and the reduction of blood flow to the skin. The dermis ultimately becomes deficient in essential nutrients, leading to accelerated aging. This process of aging is accompanied by the discernible discoloration of the skin, as well as the formation of wrinkles.

Impotence

Due to the vasoconstrictive effects of smoking, achieving and sustaining erections becomes more challenging. The penile blood vessels fail to undergo the necessary dilation to facilitate adequate blood flow and achieve penile rigidity, resulting in the condition of impotence. This issue impacts young male individuals who engage in smoking.

Moreover, it is a veracity that individuals who engage in cigarette smoking exhibit a diminished quantity of sperm, compounding the already distressing state of affairs. Cigarette smoking in women leads to significant fertility impediments, rendering the process of conception arduous. Females who engage in smoking require a greater duration of time in their attempts to conceive a child. When two individuals engaging in smoking habits come into contact with each other, the likelihood of conception decreases significantly.

The aforementioned are merely a few of the immediate physiological consequences that arise from cigarette smoking. It is crucial to acknowledge, however, that upon cessation of smoking, a substantial reduction in these effects, including certain enduring impacts, is observed, as the body gradually goes through a process of recuperation.

When to stop smoking

Taking the aforementioned into consideration, it is plausible that certain individuals who smoke may desire to cease their smoking habit. Nevertheless, it is crucial to acknowledge that nicotine is a profoundly addictive substance, rendering the act of quitting exceedingly challenging. Determining an exact moment to cease smoking is an elusive task, yet it is of utmost importance to emphasize that every moment represents an apt time to quit smoking. The plethora of health hazards to which smokers typically subject themselves indicate that these risks can be mitigated through cessation. Consequently, this implies that whenever you opt to cease, you will have made the correct decision.

A considerable number of individuals who smoke face challenges in successfully discontinuing the habit as a result of the profound dependence typically induced by the presence of nicotine in their body and brain. Their capacity to operate is constrained in the absence of smoking, and persistent impulses and yearnings exacerbate the challenge of cessation. Cravings denote the persistent episodes in which individuals attempting to quit smoking experience a compelling inclination to engage in smoking, particularly following meals and/or during intervals. Conversely, a compulsion pertains to situations in which the smoker is irresistibly compelled to engage in smoking due to an inexplicable sensation.

Hence, it is advisable that smokers refrain from attempting cessation during periods of heightened stress, as such circumstances commonly precipitate relapse. The presence of stress amplifies the intensity of cravings and compulsions, thereby augmenting the pressure experienced by individuals attempting to quit smoking. When making the decision to engage in smoking, it is advisable to establish a network of acquaintances consisting of friends and family members, who can provide valuable support, aiding in adherence to one's chosen path and assisting in effectively managing the accompanying societal pressures. Nevertheless, it should be noted that relapses do not signify ultimate failure, but rather provide valuable opportunities for learning. Typically, it requires smokers multiple attempts, sometimes as many as five or beyond, to successfully overcome the habit and achieve complete liberation from cigarettes.

One effective approach to supporting individuals who smoke is by providing them with comprehensive information about the advantages of abstaining from smoking, which can serve as a powerful source of motivation to help them overcome this hazardous habit. Despite the likelihood of their dismissal by many individuals, there will be a subset of individuals who will recognize and embrace the advantages offered by these incentives, thus utilizing them as a crucial catalyst for smoking cessation.

www.ingramcontent.com/pod-product-compliance
Lightning Source LLC
Chambersburg PA
CBHW052136110526
44591CB00012B/1738